Chuckles

(Verses to a-Muse)

To Dale,
Have a 'chuckle'
on me! All the best—
John

John F. Foster

To order additional copies of this book, contact:
Xlibris Corporation
1-888-795-4274
www.Xlibris.com
Orders@Xlibris.com
84788

Dedication

The publication of my first book, *Discovery! A Wordcrafter's Journey,* was a landmark event in my life. I dedicated it to my loving wife, Lorraine, in great appreciation for her unending patience and enthusiastic support.

It is time to acknowledge my wonderful daughter, Elizabeth Foster, with the publication of this second collection. Her appreciation of my peculiar sense of humor and her encouragement have provided inspiration to explore what talent I may have. I dedicate this book to her in sincere gratitude for her constant support and her invaluable technical know-how.

John F. Foster

Acknowledgments

In addition to acknowledging the wonderful support coming from my wife and daughter, I wish to thank readers of my work for their encouragement to publish a second collection. Not only are these close personal friends and members of several local poetry groups, but they are also fellow poets online at Poets For Integrity and World Of Poets web sites.

Additionally, I wish to extend sincere thanks to the management and staff of my publisher, XLibris, for their professionalism and expertise.

John F. Foster

This year, 2010, marks the 100th anniversary of the death of Mark Twain, one of America's great writers and humorists. It seems fitting to quote him on this occasion.

"Humor is the great thing, the saving thing. The minute it crops up, all our irritations and resentments slip away and a sunny spirit takes their place".

Mark Twain, 1835-1910

Other poetry books by John F. Foster
(available at Amazon.com)

Discovery! A Wordcrafter's Journey. A unique blend of wit and wisdom, humor and insight. A potpourri of verse forms, wordplay, and explanatory pages.

Where There's A Quill (A Poetry Pastiche), to be published in early 2011 by XLibris. An exploration of a variety of poetry forms written with themes of inspiration, regret, love, loss, joy, anger, compassion, wonder. This collection contains examples of Foster's award-winning work which bear his mark as a wordsmith.

Preface

Poetry is catching. I inhaled a serious poetic germ in 2008 and I have been sneezing out poems ever since, afflicted, smitten. A lover of words since my earliest memories, I explored this passion as a language teacher (French) and for years cranked out homemade verse in tribute to friends and family.

That serious germ floated my way in the form of a humorous poetry contest. I submitted, waited, hoped. Came up empty . . . . but full of motivation to learn more. My germ was germinating, as it were. Fellow poets on an international web site critiqued, instructed, encouraged me. I read, studied, and experimented. My first book, *Discovery! A Wordcrafter's Journey* appeared in January, 2009.

Since publication, I have had the privilege of sharing my work with dozens of civic clubs, literary groups, libraries and nursing home residents. Because these audiences seem to prefer my light, humorous verses—poems with a certain wit, whimsy, wordplay—I have assembled these particular efforts into one volume. The poems in *Chuckles* represent a variety of forms, as you will note in the Poetry Reference Pages. I have included a few favorites (marked by an asterisk) from my first book to attract interest among new readers in that volume.

Some of the humor in this book is not original. In these cases, as with all of my work, the versification is mine.

A final note: You will encounter a number of short verses known as senryu (sen-ree-yoo). This is a Japanese form of three lines similar to the haiku (see Poetry Reference Pages). Senryu may appear simplistic, but are traditionally crafted to offer concise observations in seventeen syllables about the human condition. The three lines of the senryu are customarily arranged in a 5-7-5 syllable count.

John F. Foster

Contents

Poetry Reference Pages

Higgledy-Piggledy—Otherwise known as a double dactyl (dah/dit/dit/dah/dit/dit meter) this form has a rigid structure and is usually humorous. It contains two stanzas in which the final lines rhyme. The first line of the first stanza is repetitive nonsense (look for clues to the theme). The second line is the subject of the poem, usually someone's name. Note that the name must itself be a double dactyl (dah/dit/dit/dah/dit/dit). There is also a requirement for at least one line of the second stanza to be a single double dactyl word. British/American in origin, this form was popularized in the late 19th century by Anthony Hecht and John Hollander.

Limerick—A five-line stanza, humorous, with strict rhyme scheme and accentual rhythm of two short syllables followed by one long syllable. Rhyming is aabba.

McWhirtle—A light verse similar to the Higgledy-Piggledy invented in 1989 by the American poet Bruce Newling. The McWhirtle adds an extra unstressed syllable at the beginning of each stanza. Syllables may move from the end of one line to the beginning of the next for readability. Dactyl meter. Usually humorous.

Senryu—(pronounced sen-ree-yoo) An unrhymed Japanese poem composed traditionally of seventeen syllables. It usually consists of three lines with a syllable count of 5-7-5. The senryu is similar to the haiku form, except that it relates to human beings rather than to nature. Hence, themes can be playful, satiric or humorous, unlike in most haiku poetry.

Tanka—An ancient Japanese verse of 31 syllables, said to be the most popular form of poetry in Japan for at least 1300 years. Style and themes have changed over the years from expressions of passion and heartache, and now include modern language, colloquialisms and even humor. In Japanese, tanka are often written in one straight line, but in English and other languages, the lines are usually divided into five syllabic units: 5-7-5-7-7.

Tetractys—A verse form consisting of five lines with syllable counts of 1-2-3-4-10. Any theme. Usually humorous. Double Tetractys verses are written in a structure that requires a reverse syllable pattern for the second verse.

Whitney—A form invented by Betty Ann Whitney, current President of the Florida State Poets Association. It is a seven-line poem with a syllable structure of 3-4-3-4-3-4-7. Rhyming optional. Any theme.

For Sale

Beneath its shadow he sits,
sweat glistening iridescent
in colors of the yawning beach umbrella
perched over his orange pick-up.

Like a bin of beach balls, the watermelons,
cool-green and wiped for shine,
beckon in the heat.

The hotter the better,
he thinks wetly
and adjusts the tilt.

Corner lot,
just the spot,
Jeez, it's hot!
Have I got
melon rot?
Won't make squat . . . .

Radio drips Alabama blues
into the thirsty noonday.
Traffic zips, oblivious to his
"Watermellons A Dollar"
and his freshly painted pick-up.

No show nohow.
Nobody . . . .

Nothing.

Wait!

Bumpthump onto the grass.
Another pick-up.
Ma and Pa and
a passel of dusty kids.

"How much for the umbrella?"

Poet's Comment: Do you think he sold the umbrella? Stay tuned for the sequel in my next book.

Caught In The Middle
(tanka)

Why have middle names?
I've discovered the reason,
    thinking of children.

Sole purpose so they can tell
when they're really in trouble.

Poet's comment: "John Franklin Foster, you come here right now!"

Redundancy
(senryu)

Needless repeating
is needless, like déjà vu
all over again.

Poet's comment: etc. and so forth.

Nirvana Americana
(senryu)

Ignorance is bliss.
If so, some in Washington
apt to die of joy.

Poet's comment: As it is, as it will always be . . . .

John F. Foster

Bivalve
(double dactyl)

Hithery-Dithery
Dee Licious Cockleshell
fluttered her valves to an-
nounce she was "bi".

All the he-shells being
heterosexual,
didn't know whether to
give her a try.

Poet's comment: double-dactyls (see Poetry Reference Pages) allow for hyphenation in order to conform to strict metric requirements. Though these forms usually begin with the nonsense phrase "Higgledy-Piggledy" (and are often known by this name), I sometimes alter this initial line, creating a subtle allusion to the theme. Did you catch that?

"Open Wide!"
(limerick)

An opera singer named Keith,
to Maestro he said "If you pleath,
I'll sing allegretto
that high "C" libretto;
just find me my falsetto teeth!"

Poet's comment: . . . . waiting for the fallout.

John F. Foster

Noise Reduction
(senryu)

Newest self-help group
made for compulsive talkers:
On-And-On-Anon.

Poet's comment: I have nothing further to say.

Reintarnation
(senryu)

Coming back to life
in a completely new form
as a hillbilly.

Poet's comment: When you read "Taking a 'Shine" (later in this volume), you know it could be worse.

Age Gauge
(senryu)

what did I do with
my keys . . . . my glasses . . . . my mind
realization

Poet's comment: It seems appropriate to have forgotten the punctuation.

Q & A

Hi, Di. (Sigh)
Mai Tai? (Try)
Wi-fi? (Sly)
Aye-Aye. (Lie)
My guy? (why?)
I cry? (Dry)
Bye-bye. (Sigh)

Poet's comment: Experimental. Original, perhaps. A rendez-vous in monorhyme, leaving the reader to fill in the blanks.

Precise Advice
(senryu)

Come on, I've told you
millions and millions of times:
"Don't exaggerate!"

Poet's comment: Best advice I've ever heard.

Murphy & Company
(senryu suite)

Severity of itch—
inversely proportional
to anyone's reach.

———————————

Dialing wrong number—
never a busy signal.
Someone will answer.

———————————

Once you find products
you like, manufacturer
will stop making them.

———————————

Any tool when dropped
will become in the corner
inaccessible.

———————————

Those with reserved seats
furthest from the theater aisle
always arrive last.

Poet's comment: If we can smile through our pessimism, ...

Clothes Lines
(senryu)

Camouflage trousers
on my shopping list to buy.
Couldn't find any.

Poet's comment: Like see-through blouses?

I-con
(senryu)

One can admire
a self-made man, unless
he worships his creator.

Poet's comment: Lower case "c", of course.

John F. Foster

*Scarecrow's Lament

Crows' disrespect for him's a sin,
his efforts crops to shield,
despite the fact he's always been
outstanding in his field.

Poet's comment: I've always wanted to create a vehicle for this pun!

Spitting Image?
(senryu)

Vanity sagging.
Mirror, mirror on the wall,
what the hell happened?

Poet's comment: That's it. Spit back.

John F. Foster

Nash Nosh

Thanksgiving Day in Albuquerque,
that city with the spelling quirque.
The menu's not southwest beef jerque;
instead, a perque breast of turque.

Poet's comment: With a nod, nay a bow, to Ogden Nash.

Arachnoleptic Fit

The
frantic
dance performed
just after you've
mistakenly walked through a spider web.

Poet's comment: This poem takes the form of a tetractys (see Poetry Reference Pages). The title of this example is a neologism, a made-up word or expression. Here, the poem is its definition. Step lively!

Source

(tanka)

Legislators might
review their priorities
when water pipes break.

Much too busy mopping up
to . . . . uh . . . . shut off the water.

Poet's comment: Parallels BP in a funny way, though I wrote this one prior to the oil spill.

*Age Sensitive
(Higgledy-Piggledy)

Biggery-Diggery
Anthony Wickersham
boasts "I'm in love at age
eighty, you see.

She's a professor of
paleontology.
I know she'll love an old
fossil like me!"

Poet's comment: Tony Wickersham is an old friend (but not that old!). This poem is one of my personal favorites. Did you find a clue in Line 1?

John F. Foster

Sex
(senryu)

Sex not the answer.
Sex is really the question.
The answer is "yes".

Poet's comment: So why ask? Just get "on" with it!

Middle Age Riddle
(senryu)

Surest birth control
for middle age and beyond?
Answer: nudity.

Poet's comment: . . . . but there are light switches.

Gutter Language
(Whitney)

Raindrops grow
  into trickle,
    starting flow
      into downspout
        to tickle
          slumbering frog.
            Wakes up, hops into shower.

Poet's comment: Playing with shape, imagery and an unusual syllable count (see Whitney in Poetry Reference Pages). *Note*: Since writing this poem, I have learned that the inventor of the form, Betty Ann Whitney, current President of the Florida State Poets Association, lives nearby. I have since joined her chapter of the FSPA.

Writers' Caveats
(senryu)

Remember two things:
avoid clichés like the plague;
never use "never".

Poet's comment: I'll never remember to avoid clichés like the plague.

John F. Foster

Oh, Fudge!
(senryu)

Mix sugar, cocoa,
butter, walnuts and you get . . . .
terminal acne.

Poet's comment: Chocoholics and dermatologists, unite!

Passion Rationale

Snowy mountain
(whipping cream)
starts you countin' . . . .
Doesn't seem
like too many
calories.
Is there any
reason, please,
why you shouldn't
just indulge?
Oh, but wouldn't
tummy bulge?

Don't insert
a pang of guilt!
(With dessert,
your will will wilt!)
Don't resist
the mound's allure.
Just insist
the cream is pure.

Got to wish
with guiltless scream,
"Pile my dish
with whipping cream!"

Face temptation,
mountaineer!
Take vacation,
lick your fear!

Mountain will
no longer threaten.
Eat your fill
without regrettin'!

Poet's comment: As they say, "I can resist anything except temptation."

Kindling
(senryu)

Should I put fire
into all my poetry?
No, quite the reverse.

Poet's comment: The dreaded retort.

John F. Foster

Christmas Greetings
(senryu)

Before its "Hello",
Christmas is saying "Buy! Buy!"
Buy now, pray later.

Poet's comment: Alas.

Wordplay (puzzle)
(tanka)

Letters in "new door"
can be made into one word.
A worthy challenge.

Try before reading ahead . . . .

(go back to line 2: "one word").

Poet's comment: Having fun with words. At your expense, of course.

*Foreplay

She tilts her head back knowingly,
awaiting his caress,
and eyes his fingers glowingly,
desire to express.

She inches forward proffering
her nape for tender touch,
her body writhing, offering
the charms he loves so much.

His musky scent intoxicates;
she moans in ecstasy.
Her warmth upon him radiates
her physicality.

He blows a whisper in her ear
while tickling at her chin.
Her shiver at his voice so near
brings on a knowing grin.

He gently carries her to bed
and turns off hallway light.
He pats her on her feline head,
then bids his cat good night.

Poet's comment: Did I hear heavy breathing?

Teens' Genes

Adolescent
moments opportune—
somnolescent
'til the crack of noon!

Poet's comment: Years ago, I was a skilled practitioner.

John F. Foster

Marital Judgment
(senryu)

I never question
my wife's judgment—after all,
look whom she married.

Poet's comment: I have not shared this poem with my wife, and hope she overlooks it here.

Up And Away!
(McWhirtle)

Deep down in the cannon was
Clarence The Cannonball,
ready to dazzle the crowd
with his grit.

Kaboom! Out the barrel, he
overshot safety net,
finding his dream to become
A "smash hit"!

Poet's comment: Like the Higgledy-Piggledy, the McWhirtle (see Poetry Reference Pages) has similar cadence and rhyme but is not quite so filled with strict requirements.

Circles
(senryu)

Some politicians
may have two oars in water,
but both on same side.

Poet's comment: Forecast: maelstrom!

Gaffe
(senryu)

"Traditionally,
most of Australia's imports
come from overseas".

Poet's comment: Words spoken by a former Australian cabinet minister. I couldn't resist using this quote as his words fit perfectly into the 5-7-5 format of a senryu.

Spotcha! Gotcha!
(Higgledy-Piggledy)

Teachery-Featury
Portia Lee Paranoid
had sev'ral eyes in the
back of her head,

thereby reducing the
classroom shenanigans.
"Omnidirectional
radar", she said.

Poet's comment: I had a third grade teacher (partially paranoid) who always seemed to know what was going on while facing the blackboard. Re. this poetic form (see Poetry Reference Pages), contrary to tradition, I'm concocting a first line which alludes to the theme.

Phone Drone
(senryu)

Menu selection:
choose from following options,
none of them human.

**Poet's comment: Caught in a revolving door. Finally escape
in order to talk to a wall.**

Subtle Maneuver
(senryu)

Looking down and out.
Can I get used to my space,
walking in this suit?

Poet's comment: Pushing the envelope here, with something of a double entendre. If I had used a hyphen after "space" instead of a comma, would you have read the poem differently? In that case, I suppose I could have changed the title to "Shuttle Maneuver".

Tasting The Waters

Warmest pools, her summer eyes.
Liquid gems, to some, her eyes.
Thirsty thoughts, in sum, arise.
"Bottoms up!", to summarize.

Poet's comment: I'll drink to that!

John F. Foster

Self-ish

(senryu)

Searched for simile
for my "self"—too much ego!
Removed "i", found smile.

Poet's comment: We often do best to remove the "I".

Age Gauge II
(tetractys)

It's
scary
when you start
making the same
kinds of noises as your coffee maker.

Poet's comment: "Oh, did you put the coffee on, dear?"

John F. Foster

Indecision
(senryu)

My uncertainty.
Is it a good or bad thing?
Can't make up my mind.

Poet's comment: Six of one . . . .

A New Dance
(senryu)

"The Politician".
Two steps forward, one step back,
and then a side step.

Poet's comment: From backroom to ballroom (and back).

Groaner
(limerick)

A foggy old fogy named Cyrus,
Whose health was far less than desirous,
Cried "It might be the flu,
Though I haven't a clue,
Unless it's the old 'C-Nile' virus!"

Poet's comment: 'pun my word!

Crossword Clue
(senryu)

Sheep's clothing for wolf,
or Runyonesque expression:
Answer: ewe's guise.

Poet's comment: Sound it out.

*A Light Touch

Her husband reaches 'neath the sheets.
She sighs at his first touch.
His hand descends—her heart skips beats,
she loves his touch so much.
His fingers further down then drop;
his quest is urgent now.
She groans and pleads "Oh, please don't stop!"
He stops. She wonders . . . . How?!?
"Hey honey, why'd you quit so soon?",
her voice a puzzled note.
He answers, humming to a tune:
"I found it—the remote".

Poet's comment: Referring to the above, you may believe that I've been accused on many occasions of writing a disappointing poem.

Rationalysis
(tanka)

Don't call me lazy.
I say "Why even bother?"
My philosophy:

If something were worth doing,
'twould have been done already.

Poet's comment: An inconvenient convenience.

John F. Foster

"High" Minded
(tanka)

Oh, of course, that's right!
You have no time for others
in your coke-quest to

be "one with the universe"
(on a scale of one to ten).

Poet's comment: Enough said.

Five Minutes To Curtain

Find place on stage. Relax and concentrate.
Just close my eyes; it might facilitate
and help to find my character . . . . but I
should still have known I needed some shut-eye
instead of worrying that I might falter
and running lines all night on the phone with wimpy Walter.

Of course that clunkhead stinks more than he knows.
He missed his entrance, then burst in and froze.
Dropped half a page of lines and couldn't cover,
so I ad-libbed his scene (as the mad lover!)

Wow! Listen to the crowd, the house is packed.
I've got to settle down, or be attacked
by dreaded butterflies. Cold sweat sets in—
must fight the influx of adrenaline.

So tense! . . . . What am I doing here? Good grief!
And where is Jill? Oh, there. What a relief!
Who else? Oh, no! We're missing Cheryl!
That op'ning love scene will be rather sterile!

How much more time before the curtain rises
(and we begin an evening of . . . . "surprises")?
One last deep breath, that's what I've got to take
and try to minimize just what's at stake.

But I can't breathe! Oh Lord, there goes the curtain
just when I'm achin' and I'm hurtin"!
The stage lights hit me and I feel like screaming . . . .
The nightmare stops. I've only just been dreaming.

Poet's comment: As an actor in community theater, I've been there . . . .

Wrangle Angle
(senryu)

Family disputes
gain perspective stepping back.
It's all relative.

Poet's comment: Feud for thought.

John F. Foster

Driver's Ed
(tanka)

Picked up for speeding,
89-year-old's excuse:
"I had to get here

somehow before I forgot
where on earth I was going!"

Poet's comment: Makes perfectly good sense to me.

Anagram Inanity
(tanka)

What equals thirteen?
"Twelve plus one" or it might be
"eleven plus two".

Either way, each phrase contains
exactly the same letters.

Poet's comment: It's nonsense like this that keeps me awake at night. Now, maybe I can doze off . . . .

John F. Foster

*Male Attachment
(senryu)

Florida lovebugs,
mating airborne spring and fall.
Spy one, get one free!

Poet's Comment: Two for the price of one. On the wind, and on the windshields!

The Shin Bone
(senryu)

A handy device
used for finding furniture
in a darkened room.

Poet's comment: Ouch!

John F. Foster

Until?
(senryu)

My resolution:
never to procrastinate,
I promise; just wait!

Poet's comment: For me in the military, it was "Hurry up and wait". Since my discharge, it's been "Wait, then hurry up!

Taking A 'Shine
(senryu)

Sunflowers guzzle
sunshine, much as hillbillies
chug-a-lug moonshine.

Poet's comment: I'm reminded of the lines from two familiar songs: "The hills are alive . . . ." "In the still of the night . . . ."

John F. Foster

(Ad)vice-versa
(senryu)

Handing out advice.
Fine—until people seek to
return the favor.

Poet's comment: Take my advice . . . .

*Name Claim

Note: I have long been a collector of remarkable names of real people. The names presented in this poem, for all their wondrous strangeness, are honest-to-goodness names of our fellow Americans. God bless 'em!

Precious Darling, Precious Jewel . . . .
Parents weren't so very cruel.
These are names quite glorious,
unlike some uproarious
monikers like Ozark Hill,
Erna Dollar, Dollar Bill,
Fuller Beans and Ginger Ale,
Raynor Shine and Never Fail,
Phelan Young, and Anna Gramm,
O. Howe Goode, Virginia Hamm.
Don't these two fit like a glove:
True Bridegroom and Skillful Love?
Makes you wonder why they christen
with these names. Do parents listen?

Poet's comment: Take a bow, folks!